Walking in the Prophetic

Embracing and Walking in Today's

Prophetic Revolution

EXPANDED EDITION

By: *Dennis Paul Goldsworthy-Davis*

Open Wells Ministries

15315 Capital Port

Sam Antonio, TX 78249

www.openwellsministries.org

PREFACE

My Introduction to the Realm of the Prophetic

One of my first experiences in the realm of the prophetic actually came before I made Jesus Lord of my life. I responded to an appeal in a Christian camp but had not yet experienced His Lordship. One night, at the age of 17, I dreamt of an old girlfriend. I woke from the dream and knew she would be my wife. Here was the problem: I had not seen her for several years. We had gone on separate paths. Yet when I met her again (quite by accident) several years later, she was going to church to keep her mum happy. I came alongside, was born again and married all in three months. I believe that we are truly heirs of salvation before we have yet responded to the Lord because God in his foreknowledge knows we will respond.

Another experience came just a few months after I was born again. I was standing in my mother-in-law's front room and suddenly saw myself in a vision. I was standing on a platform. The auditorium was large and semicircular, rather like the auditoriums of today. I was speaking and I could feel the power of God. What is so wild is that to that time (just four months into salvation), I had never experienced the power of God. But in this vision I knew what it was! God was, of course, showing me my call into the ministry.

These experiences came when I prayed and worshipped but nobody back in the 1970's really knew enough about the prophetic or the prophet's office to explain to me what was happening. I was part of a movement that really only catered to pastors and teachers. Only later did I understand my call to the prophetic office.

From that time on I began to pray that God would use me in the gifts of the Spirit and also confirm my call into the ministry. The confirmation of His call was so specific that it bears mention at this time.

I had read a book on Smith Wigglesworth and was deeply moved. He suggested a second prayer time in the day so, added to my morning prayer, I began to pray for a short time after supper at night. One night after such a prayer time I readied myself to leave the room when I heard the voice of God say, "Do not leave My presence, son.". Shocked, I stayed! The next few nights I worshipped and prayed and had such an invasion of the Holy Spirit accompanied with the presence of angels, it was amazing. Then one night the King Himself stepped in. I experienced the awe, the wonder, the presence! While in that moment I heard a voice so loud and yet within me that said, "Whom shall I send? Who will go for me?". I was dumbfounded. I looked around to see who He was talking to! "Surely not me, Lord? Yes, me!" I had received my confirmation and my call into the prophetic office. What made it more amazing is that the next day a seasoned minister came 'round for supper. He had been staying in town for a few days of rest. When I told him what had happened he confirmed by sharing that was exactly how he himself was called by God.

My journey was on! Bible school next? No. The Lord spoke to me clearly from 1 John 2:27 that I was going to be taught by the anointing Himself. What a journey! What a beginning! This book contains some of my revelations along the way and some guidelines that might help individuals and churches to walk in this wonderful realm.

Dennis

OTHER BOOKS BY
DENNIS PAUL GOLDSWORTHY-DAVIS

Available on Amazon.com

Grace Looks Good on You

Touching the God of Jacob

Standing in the Perfect Storm

Gaining the Commanded Blessings

Unlimited Anointing: Secrets to Operating in the Fullness of God's Power

EXPANDED Edition

©2022 by Open Wells Ministries

No part of this book, written or graphic, may be reproduced by any means whatsoever, mechanical or electronic, without written permission from the publisher,
Open Wells Ministries, 15315 Capital Port, San Antonio, TX 78249

Library of Congress Number:

ISBN: 978-1-7355716-4-5

Printed in the United States of America by Open Wells Ministries

Scripture references were taken from:

THE HOLY BIBLE, NEW INTERNATIONAL VERSION®, NIV® Copyright © 1973, 1978, 1984, 2011 by Biblica, Inc.® Used by permission. All rights reserved worldwide.

KING JAMES VERSION

REFERENCES ARE PUBLIC DOMAIN IN THE US

TABLE OF CONTENTS

Foreword by Robert Henderson…………………….. 11
Introduction…………………………………………... 13
Chapter 1 – The Basis of the Prophetic…………… 15
Chapter 2 – Realms of the Prophetic……………… 21
Chapter 3 – Importance of Prophecy……………… 28
Chapter 4 – Understanding the Times……………. 31
Chapter 5 – The Power of the Word of God……… 34
Chapter 6 – The War Against the Word…………... 36
Chapter 7 – Learning to Prophesy………………… 39
Chapter 8 – Overcoming Obstacles to Prophecy….. 43
Chapter 9 – The Character Needed to Prophesy….. 47
Chapter 10 – Learning Prophetic Etiquette………… 52
Chapter 11 – Responding to a Word from God…….. 56
Chapter 12 – The Violent Take it by Force………… 64
Chapter 13 – Wrong Reactions to the Prophetic…… 66
Chapter 14 – The Making of a Prophet……………... 69
Chapter 15 – The Arch Enemy of the Prophetic……. 73
Chapter 16 – Keys to a Prophetic Lifestyle………… 76
Chapter 17 – The Ways of God……………………… 79
Conclusion 82
Testimonials.. 83
Biography……………………………………….…..… 85

FOREWORD
BY ROBERT HENDERSON

Dennis Goldsworthy-Davis is a true governmental prophet of the Lord. Many times, as he has been invited into the apostolic center that I led, he has brought not just a word of the Lord, but the directional, confirming word of God to me and the house. On a personal level, the Lord has used Dennis to speak in times of transition, a word that has brought courage and encouragement to go after the fresh thing that God was doing. I esteem Dennis to be a prophet of the Lord for the times we live in. I recommend him highly to any ministry and/or church that is seeking to hear the voice of the Lord.

In addition, there is a cry in people's hearts to experience the true prophetic. We are moving into a new season of prophetic revelation. Dennis brings a history and wealth of prophetic integrity to help us transition into these seasons. There are new dimensions of the prophetic opening in the spirit realm. Dennis and his wisdom can strengthen us as we navigate into these new places. With these new seasons come great opportunities to encounter God and spiritual realities in the unseen realm. With these opportunities comes the need to understand prophetic protocol. Dennis as a seasoned prophet helps us move in the spirit and access the places God has ordained for us to walk.

-Robert Henderson

INTRODUCTION

Today is a day of unparalleled times in the body of Christ. We have seen throughout this last century a restoration of so many things. This truly is a fulfillment of the scripture that Peter was speaking of in Acts 3:21, "A time when God restores all things." Yet, there is a principle of restoration that is clearly seen: *The last thing lost is the first thing restored and the first thing lost is the last thing restored.* This principle can be seen through history to be so true time after time. You can clearly see this in the teachings and experiences of salvation, baptism, etc.

In this restorative process we have been awaiting two major issues: The restoration of the prophet and the restoration of the apostle. When these two offices are fully restored to the church, we will be ready for the great latter-day outpouring of the Holy Spirit as described in the book of Joel.

It is clear that the day of restoration of the prophet has come! As in all cases of restoration, extremes have come with it. It is my clear desire, in the writing of this book, to bring an understanding and a balance during this time of the prophet's restoration. Many books have already been written regarding the prophetic, but often only covering certain aspects. My goal is to help create a balanced understanding therefore enabling the reader to understand the prophetic process and response.

CHAPTER 1
The Basis of the Prophetic

When we read the first words of the first book of the Bible, Genesis, several things instantly stand out!

>*"In the beginning God…"* Genesis 1:1

>*"In the beginning God created…"* Genesis 1:1

>*"In the beginning…the Spirit of God was hovering…"* Genesis 1:2

>*"In the beginning…God said…"* Genesis 1:3

And it was so!

He who was in the beginning spoke and released his voice, the Holy Spirit hovered waiting for his voice and when his voice was released the Holy Spirit moved to fulfill the word that was released. God said and it was so.

In the beginning God prophesied, *"Let there be…"*. It released the creative power of the word. *"…and it was so."* God believed in himself and believed in his word and the Holy Spirit reacted. This began the operation of the prophetic throughout creation and creation became a reality. But God did not keep his speaking to himself. He began to not only speak to man but speak through man. It seems through scriptural reading that both Enoch and Noah were prophetic and prophesied. Noah prophesied at least by action and Enoch by word, too.

> *"Enoch, the seventh from Adam, prophesied about them..."* Jude 1:14.

God was establishing a precedent not just of him speaking sovereignly but speaking through man with awesome results! Ezekiel 37, in the passage of the dry bones, revealed the awesome power of what happens when men prophesy as commanded or led.

> *"So I prophesied as he commanded me, and breath entered them; they came to life and stood up on their feet—a vast army."* Ezekiel. 37:10.

Reinhard Bonnke gave such a beautiful illustration when preaching in Africa of how the Lord explained to him that God's word in his mouth was as powerful as God's word in God's mouth. The key was the word of God itself! That is how powerful the prophetic can be.

In the New Testament we read that when the disciples preached the word of God, the Holy Spirit went with them and confirmed the word with signs.

> *"Then the disciples went out and preached everywhere, and the Lord worked with them and confirmed his word by the signs that accompanied it."* Mark 16:20.

The Holy Spirit was operating and ministering when the word was spoken. So, nothing has changed! The Holy Spirit still moves on the release of the Word of the Lord.

Yes indeed, a precedent has been set. God speaks and the Holy Spirit moves. Added to that, God speaks through men not only in preaching but in prophecy and the Holy Spirit moves when God is the author of the prophetic! To truly understand the prophetic now we fully understand its origin and where its source lies.

As God's people, we are in desperate need of the prophetic so that we do not suffer destruction or ruin in the hour we live in. The Bible says,

> *"...my people are destroyed from lack of knowledge."* Hosea 4:6

Verse 14 goes on to say,

> *"...a people without understanding will come to ruin!"* Hosea 4:14

It is imperative to understand that God is the origin of all prophecies. Peter states:

> *"For prophecy never had its origin in the human will, but prophets, though human, spoke from God as they were carried along by the Holy Spirit."* 2 Peter 1:21

This will teach us the most important and basic of lessons in the prophetic:

- God is the author of all prophecy.
- The Holy Spirit is the agent of all prophecy
- Men are only conduits of the prophetic. Not the source!
- The Holy Spirit must be operative in the life of prophecy.

Critical to our understanding is,

> *"Above all, you must understand that no prophecy of Scripture came about by the prophet's own interpretation of things."* 2 Peter 1:20

There is a dangerous trait being taught regarding the prophetic in today's church. It states that a prophet can prophesy at will. Scripture clearly does not back this! Unfortunately, this will lead to error and will not keep the prophetic pure! God is the origin of prophecy, not us.

Prophets can only prophesy what God speaks to them and shows them! In fact, the Greek word used for *prophesy* actually means *to break forth under inspiration.*

While we deeply desire the true pure flow of the prophetic, scripture clearly teaches that there are some wrong sources that can give rise to incorrect words and revelations. Here are Bible references for those wrong sources:

- One's own imagination. Ezekiel 3:2

- One's own spirit. Ezekiel 13:3…God actually calls these lies

- One's own mind. Jeremiah 23:16…in verse 26 of the same chapter the Lord speaks of *"…delusions of their mind."*

- One's own stubborn heart. Jeremiah 23:17

- Stolen prophecies. Jeremiah 23:30

- Plain lies. Jeremiah 23:25

- Another spirit. Jeremiah 23:13

While there are false sources of the prophetic, Scripture clearly gives us true and valid sources of the prophetic. True prophecy will flow from these sources:

- From his presence! Jeremiah 23:18

- It can be either seen or heard! Jeremiah 23:18

Now this hearing of the prophetic source can come in varying ways as the Lord determines to give it. The hearing may come by:

- Hearing a voice either audibly or in your spirit

- Hearing by an angel

The seeing of the prophetic can equally come in varying ways:

- Seeing in a dream

- Seeing in a vision
- Seeing through an actual visitation of the Lord or the Angelic

What is important to remember in all of this is the common thread which is the presence of the Lord. No matter the method He uses to speak, there will always be the sense of His presence! Alongside this common thread is that which happens in your own spirit. Whether you are the giver or the receiver of the prophetic word, there should always be a witness of the Holy Spirit confirming that which is prophesied.

CHAPTER 2
Realms of the Prophetic

As imperative as it is to understand the origins of the prophetic, it is equally critical for us to understand the differing realms in the prophetic. Let us look at and discuss the various prophetic realms that directly impact us.

First let us examine the differences between the prophet and the prophetic office in the Old and New Testament:

The Realm of the Prophetic in the Old Testament:
While the basics of the prophetic operate the same in both testaments, the operation of the "prophetic office" differs. The Old Testament Prophet heard God for the people. This came as a direct result of the people's own decision. We read that the people said,

> *"Speak to us yourself and we will listen. But do not have God speak to us or we will die."* Exodus 20:19

From this point on, this became the people's habit, therefore, they would seek a prophet out to be able to hear from God. In the New Testament a brand-new standard is set!

> *"For those who are led by the Spirit of God are children of God."* Romans 8:14

This is why in the New Testament we read over and over again Jesus continually saying, *"Whoever has ears, let them hear...".*

Here is a critical point for all believers to grasp: In the Old Testament the prophet spoke for God to the people whereas, in the New Testament God will speak to individuals and other ministry gifts!

In the Old Testament the prophet many times operated within a governmental role in their prophesying. Moses, who was clearly described as a prophet, equally had governmental rule. Samuel, though raised in a priestly office, would bring a rule into the prophetic order like no other! While the New Testament prophet can and will have governmental roles, their sphere of rule will be interlinked with the other five-fold ministry gifting as described in Ephesians.

> *"So Christ himself gave the apostles, the prophets, the evangelists, the pastors and teachers..."*
> Ephesians 4:11

Often these prophetic ministries will flow under the auspices of apostolic gifting.

John the Baptist appeared on the scene preparing the way for Jesus. John would be the last of the old order of the prophetic, giving way to the new prophetic order that Jesus would release. This is why Jesus stated,

> *"Truly I tell you, among those born of women there has not risen anyone greater than John the Baptist; yet whoever is least in the kingdom of heaven is greater than he."* Matthew 11:11

This change would signify a release of a new standard in the prophetic ministry!

Jesus himself would become the New Testament Standard for the prophetic office and ministry! Hence the incredible statement,

> *"....For it is the Spirit of prophecy who bears testimony to Jesus."* Revelation 19:10

It is this Jesus that is boldly described in this manner:

> *"When He ascended on high, he took many captives and gave gifts to His people."* Ephesians 4:9

Those precious gifts included the office of the prophet! Equally Jesus, in dramatic fashion, released the precious Holy Spirit which imparted the gift and spirit of prophecy to His people. This new standard of the prophetic ministry is what we should reach for. However, many today are still looking to the Old Testament for their prophetic models, hence releasing a wrong spirit. In all prophetic ministries we must continually reach to operate within and minister from the standard that Jesus has released to us!

The Realm of the Prophetic in the New Testament:
This realm releases three very clear prophetic ministries.

1. The motivational gifting of the prophetic: Romans 12:4-8 gives us a list of charisma or grace giftings that build the body of Christ. One of these motivational or grace gifts is that of prophecy. This gifting is essential to the building of the body of Christ!

2. The prophetic gift of the Holy Spirit: This gift described in 1 Corinthians 12:10 is essential to the body of Christ. According to 1 Corinthians 14:3, the gift of prophecy will have three flows to it:

- Edification
- Encouragement
- Comfort

Again, it is important to remember that the outworking of this gift is essential to the people of God and builds the church up!

3. The office of a prophet: It is essential to separate the office of a prophet named in Ephesians 4 from the previous two giftings. In the New Testament we see these offices operating in two important roles and functions:

- In a governmental fashion
- As a seer

Operating in a Governmental Fashion is essential for the house of God to have right foundations.

> *"...built on the foundation of the apostles and prophets, with Christ Jesus himself as the chief cornerstone."* Ephesians 2:20

Operating as a seer is the outworking of the prophetic office. This side of the prophetic office is beautifully described in the life of a man named Agabus, who spoke into events and personal lives of others.

> *"During this time some prophets came down from Jerusalem to Antioch. One of them, named Agabus, stood up and through the Spirit predicted that a severe famine would spread over the entire Roman world...."* Acts 11:27-28
>
> *"After we had been there a number of days, a prophet named Agabus came down from Judea. Coming over to us, he took Paul's belt, tied his own hands and feet with it and said, 'the Holy Spirit says, "In this way the Jewish leaders in Jerusalem will bind the owner of this belt and will hand him over to the Gentiles."* Acts 21:10-11

In looking at the differing sides of the prophetic office it is clear that one side seems to operate in a governmental / building fashion and that the seer tends to speak into events and personal lives. Many times we will see a governmental or foundational prophet as a preaching prophet. This is not necessarily true of a seer prophet. The prophetic office (both governmental and seer) is distinguished from the motivation and gift of prophecy by one clear item: revelation! The office of the prophet tends to carry more an authority and revelatory side to its outworking!

Now let us examine prophecy in individual, corporate and church life:

The Realm of the Spirit of Prophecy
The realm of the spirit of prophecy is found in Revelation and can operate in an individual (normally a prophet) or in a corporate setting.

> *"...For it is the Spirit of prophecy who bears testimony to Jesus."* Revelation 19:10

Many times the spirit of prophecy can be seen to fall in a corporate meeting where all will come under the influence of the prophetic spirit! Biblically, we see this happening when Saul meets a group of prophets and the prophetic spirit overwhelms both the company of prophets and even Saul himself.

> *"...As you approach the town, you will meet a procession of prophets coming down from the high place....and they will be prophesying. The Spirit of the Lord will come powerfully upon you, and you will prophesy with them..."* 1 Samuel 10:5-6

The Realm of the Prophetic Church
The last realm of the prophetic is that of a prophetic church. Many times churches that are led by a governmental prophet will have this strong prophetic flavor. Equally, you will notice that the message and the music that flow from these houses will have a peculiar prophetic flow to them! These churches will produce more prophetic gifting within their midst. Also, these churches will have a clear understanding of the present time the

church at large is in. A fascinating Biblical example of this is found in the church located in Antioch.

> *"Now in the church at Antioch there were prophets and teachers… While they were worshiping the lord and fasting, the Holy Spirit said, 'Set apart for me Barnabas and Saul for the work which I have called them.' So after they had fasted and prayed, they placed their hands on them and sent them off."*
> Acts 13:1-3

This church was found to be full of certain prophets and teachers. While this church had a strong teaching flavor, it equally had a great emphasis on the hearing and obeying of the Word of the Lord. You can see this response in Acts 13 during the sending of Paul and Barnabas for their missionary journeys. Clearly, Antioch had become a major prophetic house of its time!

CHAPTER 3
The Importance of Prophecy

The desperate need for prophecy in the church is spelled out over and over again in the New Testament! It is an issue of deep importance for the church during this present hour, just as it was for the New Testament church. The New Testament bears out the importance of the prophetic flow. Here are some New Testament (and Old) points to ponder and references:

- We are told to desire prophecy above all gifts!
  1 Corinthians 14:4

- Prophecy builds the church!
  1 Corinthians 14:4

- Prophecy helps men with the issues of life by strengthening, comforting and encouraging!
  1 Corinthians 14:3

- Prophecy reveals the secrets of men's hearts!
  1 Corinthians 14:24-25 Equally, this can be seen in Peter's rebuke of Ananias and Sapphira in Acts 5.

- Prophecy is for all and all can operate in this gift!
  1 Corinthians 14:31 (This is the only gift mentioned that all can operate in.)

- Prophecy reveals God's purposes for men!
  Amos 3:7

- We are commanded to never despise the gift of prophecy! 1 Thessalonians 5:19-20

- We are implored to receive a prophet and reap a reward for the honoring of that office! Matthew 10:41

- We are told that the gift of prophecy is a key to the impartation of gifting! 1 Timothy 4:14

- Prophecy releases directives to ministries and lives! Acts 13:2-3

- Prophecy gives warnings of coming events! Acts 11:28 and Acts 21:10-11

- Prophecy strengthens the church! Acts 15:32

- Prophecy equips us for the fight! 1 Timothy 1:18

- Prophecy is used to stir us up! Haggai 1:13-14

As you can clearly see, the importance and benefit of prophecy is astounding! We must never minimize its powerful impact but must look to hear and see all that He desires to show us through the prophetic!

The Holy Spirit makes it very clear how He feels regarding the prophetic! A phrase we see the Holy Spirit repeat over and over again is,

> *"...he who has an ear, let him hear what the Spirit is saying to the churches."* Revelation 2:17

This is a critical matter and always is followed by a direct promise of reward! This must be weighed in the light of a sober warning given us in Hebrews.

> *"So, as the Holy Spirit says: "Today, if you hear His voice, do not harden your hearts as you did in the rebellion...."*. Hebrews 3:7-8

God takes His Word very seriously! This includes His present Word that He is speaking to His church! This is clearly revealed when the Father says,

> *"This is my Son, whom I love; with Him I am well pleased. Listen to Him!"* (Emphasis mine) Matthew 17:5

We are commanded to listen to His voice and that in direct relation to the present word of the Lord! Jesus reveals an amazing inheritance for the church! Speaking of the Holy Spirit, He says,

> *"...He will speak what He hears, and He will tell you what is to come. He will bring glory to me by taking from what is mine and making it known to you."* John 16:13

One of the main venues in which this revealing is done is through the prophetic word of the Lord!

CHAPTER 4
UNDERSTANDING THE TIMES

Paul writing to the Romans suddenly unleashes this gem:

> *"And do this understanding the present time, the hour has come for you to wake up from your slumber." Romans 13:11*

What is he saying? It is the job of the church to understand the times they live in, the times of the church and the times of their own lives! But how can they do this unless the prophetic is involved?

> *"God does nothing unless he first declares it through his servants the prophets." Amos 3:7*

The God who said that has not changed. He releases the prophetic word of the Lord and the Spirit of prophecy to catch the times.

Let's look at some examples of this.

The prophet, Agabus, is seen several times in the book of Acts. He speaks to the times, that a famine would hit the Roman world.

> *"One of them, named Agabus, stood up and through the Spirit predicted that a severe famine would spread over the entire Roman world." Acts 11:28*

He prophesies to Paul personally telling what would happen in Jerusalem if he went there.

> *"Coming over to us, he took Paul's belt, tied his own hands and feet with it and said, 'The Holy Spirit says, "In this way the Jewish leaders in Jerusalem will bind the owner of this belt and will hand him over to the Gentiles."'"Acts 21:11*

In the book of Revelation, we hear this statement 7 times, "He that has an ear let him hear what the Spirit is saying to the churches." The whole book is a prophetic release. God uses the prophetic to awaken us to the times.

The whole premise of this statement in Romans 13:11, is to have a people ready and prepared. The warning was and is, "Let us wake up from our slumber". Oh, this is good! He reveals that a people of slumber are unaware of what is going on. So much of the church is caught in this place, I believe. So many are just wandering along in a spiritual daze unaware of the Spirit world at all.

What is needed?

- A prophetic release by the prophets into all arenas of the times.

- A waking up to the present word of the Lord.

- An ear to hear what the Spirit is saying.

- A fervency to be doing what the Lord is doing.

- A preparation to always be ready.

This can be achieved several ways:

- Develop a walk with the Holy Spirit. After all, the Bible does state

    "For those who are led by the Spirit of God are the children of God!" Romans 8:14

    "Since we live by the Spirit, let us keep in step with the Spirit." Galatians 5:25

- Get around genuine prophetic people or prophetic churches. This will help intensely. Invite bonafide prophets to minister in your churches.

I believe understanding the present times is imperative to life and to churches. The church should be on the cutting edge and not following the traits of the world.

CHAPTER 5
The Power of the Word of God

In our understanding and outworking of the prophetic it is imperative that we fully realize the power of the prophetic! Key to this understanding is this: The power of prophecy is closely tied to the power of the word of God! Let's take a brief look at references to the incredible power of God's word! By His Word:

- He created! *"And God said..."* Genesis 1:3

- He sustains all things! Hebrews 1:3

- He heals! Psalm 107:20 / Matthew 8:8

- He delivers! Luke 8:29

- He accomplishes His purposes! Isaiah 55:11

- There is more power than a two-edged sword! Hebrews 4:12

- He changes men from within! Psalm 105:19

- His Word is always confirmed supernaturally! Mark 16:20

As we consider that awesome power of the word of God, it is critical that we understand that any true prophetic word or utterance carries that same power! What truly makes any prophecy powerful has more to do with the word itself than the mouth that speaks it. One example of this is

Ezekiel. In Ezekiel chapter 37 we find the prophet speaking to dry bones what God had commanded him to speak. Through his obedience an incredible miracle took place. Again, it wasn't the mouth that spoke the word but rather the word itself! Many years ago I sat under the ministry of Reinhardt Bonnke as he revealed to us a life changing statement that the Lord had made to him. As Reinhardt stood to speak at the beginning of his ministry the Lord said to him, "My word in your mouth, Reinhardt, is the same as My word in My mouth!"

As Reinhardt embraced this powerful reality and began to speak, many were healed and delivered! Can you now see that powerful working of God's word and its impact in the prophetic realm? This is perhaps why, more than any other reason, we need to endeavor to bring such clarification and purity to the prophetic realm!

CHAPTER 6
The War Against the Word

To fully understand the importance of the prophetic we must understand how intensely Satan wars against that word! This war against God's word has been in play since the very beginning.

Let's consider two instances that clearly show Satan's vehement assault on the word of God! The first instance of Satan's words to mankind is found in Genesis.

> *"Now the serpent was more crafty than any of the wild animals the Lord God had made. He said to the woman, 'Did God really say, ...'* Genesis 3:1

"Did God really say?" This has been his strategy to this very day! He constantly calls into question what God has spoken.

The second instance is found in the same chapter.

> *"'You will not certainly die', the serpent said to the woman."* Genesis 3:4

Not only would he question if God had spoken, but he would attempt to call God's truthfulness into disrepute. Satan would finally distort the truth of God's word so much that Adam and Eve would disobey God and lose their very inheritance. Satan's desire is twofold in this matter: to rob God of our obedience and to equally rob us of every promise and purpose of God in our lives. This, my friends, is why he challenges God's words to us with such ferocity!

This battle of lies that Satan wages has continued into the New Testament. Luke 4:1-13 reveals an epic battle between the Lord Jesus and Satan that was waged in the wilderness! Satan would ask Jesus the question, "If you are the Son of God…". Through this Satan would attempt to place doubt in the mind of Christ by calling into question the purpose and promise of the Father in His life.

Secondly, Satan would attempt to convince Christ to be disobedient by doing what He was never told to do. Alongside of this ongoing war against the word of God, we see another dangerous area. This would be the misquoting or twisting of God's revealed word. This is best seen when Satan misrepresents a promise from God attempting to lure Jesus into disobedience.

> *"…throw yourself down from here. For it is written 'He will command his angels concerning you to guard you carefully; they will lift you up in their hands, so that you will not strike your foot against a stone.'"* Luke 4:10

However, this devilish practice is also practiced by a group known as the lying prophets. We see this twisted practice at work in 1Kings 13 as an older prophet, pretending to have been spoken to by an angel, lies to a younger prophet causing him to disobey God's direct word. This would cause the young prophet to lose his ministry and very life! The enemy's scheme in this arena would also cause the destruction of King Ahab. We read that a deceiving spirit entered the mouths of the prophets. It was this lying spirit that would perpetuate the king's destruction.

These examples stress to us the importance of God's prophetic word and equally the paramount desire that it be kept pure!

While the prophetic has warfare come against it, the opposite is also true! The prophetic should be used to war against the enemy. Jesus exemplifies this as He warred with what God had said, therefore overcoming Satan and his schemes. Equally, we must learn to war with the now present word of the Lord. Paul tells Timothy,

> *"... by following the prophesies that were given, we might fight a good fight."* 1Timothy 1:18

Paul commends Timothy that this warring will enable us to, *"...hold onto faith and a good conscience."*. While Satan will assault the word of God with lies, and even look to twist its intent and meaning, we have been commanded to battle with the true and pure word of the Lord for our lives!

CHAPTER 7
Learning to Prophesy

As in all giftings of the Lord, we must learn to develop the realm we have been gifted with. We are told to

> *"...prophesy in accordance with your faith."*
> Romans 12:6

This is critical to our understanding of prophetic gifting. We must learn to grow in the realm of faith within our prophetic flow! As our faith grows within the prophetic, so our prophetic flow will increase.

Let's look at the two basic ingredients of the prophetic flow within our lives and discuss them briefly. These realms as described in 1Corinthians 12:8 are known as:

- Words of knowledge
- Words of wisdom

A word of knowledge or wisdom can come as the Lord releases knowledge and wisdom of something that He knows to a recipient. This will come in varying ways:

- An impression in the matter
- A deep knowing in the matter
- The visionary realm (A seeing in your spirit, in your mind or an open vision)

- A literal dream

- The voice of the Holy Spirit (Heard in our spirit, our mind, or even audibly. Sometimes His voice can be so loud it seems as though you heard it "out loud.")

- An angel speaks

- A quickening of scripture in the matter

In all these cases, the Holy Spirit will quicken your spirit man. When you first begin in this realm, you will many times feel your heart will explode. As we grow in these gifts, it will become a slight quickening in our spirit that we must heed.

Let's look closely now at the realm of the prophet in our desire to learn to prophesy. While the prophet will operate in words of knowledge and wisdom, there needs to be a distinction between the gifting and office of the prophetic. The largest difference we see in this realm is that of prediction and revelation. The office of the prophet will many times carry the understanding of the present times in its prophetic declaring and outworking. One of the most noticeable differences we see in the prophetic office is that prophesying will be accompanied by a clear, powerful manifestation of the Holy Spirit. This office and realm are desperately needed in today's church!

As we have previously stated the realm of faith is important as we learn to prophesy. Again, Romans 12:6

tells us we must prophesy in accordance with our faith. We must never attempt to step beyond our realm of faith in the prophetic. Those who do will move from the prophetic to something that is merely presumption. This will eventually lead us into error and sin.

> *"...everything that does not come from faith is sin."* Romans 14:23

Staying in the boundaries of our present faith is God's safeguard in our prophetic flow. In learning to prophesy we must strive to stay accountable and not become a lone wolf in our prophetic outworking.

> *"...the others should weigh carefully what is said."* 1Corinthians 14:29

If we are to legitimately grow in the prophetic we must stay accountable to church leadership and other prophetic ministries! This is a safeguard for us and others. Also, we must learn to stay subject to ourselves.

> *"The spirits of the prophets are subject to the control of the prophets."* 1Corinthians 14:32

Therefore, we must never say, "I couldn't control myself, I had to prophesy!" This is not permissible and is a violation!

Finally, in our learning to prophesy the need for true and proven prophetic mentoring is essential. Mentoring in the prophetic is very useful in gift development and, more importantly, in character development. The Old Testament reveals to us a useful pattern in mentoring of the prophetic which has a dual outworking. One, there were schools of prophets that would train prophets. Secondly, a younger prophet would walk with an older prophet growing their ministry and gifting. Both of these avenues are still just as viable today! We must be sure that whoever mentors our call and gifting has a proven track record and good report!

CHAPTER 8
Overcoming Obstacles to Prophecy

"For you can all prophesy in turn....."
1Corinthians 14:31

It is clear that all do not prophesy. In fact, most do not prophesy! The purpose of this chapter is to pull down some of the strongholds that keep individuals from prophecy. While there are numerous reasons, these we find to be the most common:

- The wrong belief system
- The feeling of unworthiness
- Fear of rejection
- Fear of failure
- Fighting off condemnation
- Past failure

Wrong belief systems hinder prophecy. The erroneous belief systems that prophecy is not for today is a very common reason folks will not enter the prophetic realm. Also, the belief that only a certain chosen few can prophesy stagnates prophetic release. Some believe that you must reach a certain level spiritually to prophesy. All these false belief systems will cripple one's ability to prophesy. The antidote to these wrong belief systems is a full return to scripture and new understanding of what God says regarding prophecy. We need to show folks how the prophetic is already working in their lives, although they may not have recognized it. This will excite folks with the reality of the prophetic and quicken their faith to step into more!

The feeling of unworthiness finds its root in wrong thinking and most likely comes from a wrong understanding of the ways of God. Just think, the Corinthian church was referred to as carnal by the Apostle Paul yet equally they were reported to come behind in no gift. This is shocking yet true. If we desire to prophesy with the confidence that Christ provides we must continually recognize our standing in Christ and not in self! Fear of Rejection is probably one of the greatest areas of stumbling in the operation of the prophetic.

> *"Fear of man will prove to be a snare...."*
> Proverbs 29:25

It is essential that we find the root cause of any fear of rejection in our lives because it will severely hinder stepping out in the prophetic. After finding the root of our rejection issue we must receive ministry to remove that root otherwise it will constantly prove to be a snare stopping any prophetic flow. The ministry of encouragement will go a long way in helping rid folks of their fear of rejection. Encouragement will set us free to step out and operate faithfully in the prophetic.

Fear of failure is crippling to the prophetic. What if it is not God? What if I mess up? These types of questions resound in someone who deals with a spirit of timidity, fearing failure before even trying. One of the greatest ways to overcome this fear is to operate safely within a prophetic group exercising prophetic gifting. As an intern operates within a prophetic group, they gain confidence as others are hearing the same things together. Constant practice is a key to building confidence in the prophetic.

Fighting off condemnation is an issue that everyone who launches out to do anything in God will face. Prophecy is no exception to that scheme of the enemy! It is essential that we come to a clear and firm understanding of condemnation's source. Romans tells us clearly that condemnation does not come from God.

> *"Therefore, there is now no condemnation for those who are in Christ Jesus…"* Romans 8:1

It has its foul origins in either the satanic or our own flesh! Remember, draw close to those with a mature prophetic gifting so that they may stand with you and ward any and every attack off. Lastly, never minister alone! We must have one another to stand strong and have encouragement.

Past failure is a part of the growing process. It is of critical importance that we remember that all ministries are like all life! Thomas Edison failed some 1100 times in attempting to invent the light bulb. He would state, "I have just learned 1100 ways not to do it." Frankly, do not take yourself so seriously that you cannot make a mistake. Forgive yourself and try again! Do not let the paralysis of failure keep you from operating in the prophetic!

Again, the list could be endless in stumbling blocks to the prophetic. However, the safeguards of good mentoring, classroom-style prophetic exercises and prophetic teams will greatly help in overcoming these areas.

CHAPTER 9
The Character Needed in the Prophetic

The prophetic realm has incredible influential power by its very nature therefore the character of those prophesying is of immense importance! This cannot be understated.

> *".... For it is the Spirit of prophecy who bears testimony to Jesus."* Revelation 19:10

Simply stated, our prophesying should speak for Jesus and turn others toward Him. Within the Bible we are warned about false prophets. Two instances speak directly to the character of those prophesying and the misrepresenting of Christ. They warn,

> *"Beware...wolves in sheep's clothing"*
> Matthew 7:15

> *"they are worldly and speak from the world."*
> 1 John 4:5

It is important to remember that Jesus said,

> *"By their fruit you will recognize them."*
> Matthew 7:16

> *"Then I will tell them plainly, 'I never knew you. Away from me, you evildoers!'"* Matthew 7:23

It appears as though these folks may have started well but went awry at some point!

It is important for us to look at some of the basic temptations that are common to the prophetic. These temptations can easily derail a prophetic person and ruin good character:

- Pride
- Independent spirit
- Sensuality
- Idolatry
- Money hungry (greed)
- Harshness
- Judgmental Spirit

Pride often comes as men exalt a prophetic ministry! Independent spirit reasoning is this; "I hear from God, who needs anyone else?"

Sensuality and sensitivity run very close together! It is of extreme importance that this be understood.

> *"Having lost all sensitivity, they have given themselves over to sensuality..."* Ephesians 4:19

Prophetic people must guard their character from moving into a "sensual" arena!

Idolatry can come many times through the adulation of a minister or ministry by others.

Money Hungry (Greed): Beware of this, as many ministries are charging for prophetic words. Some even charge differing prices for differing levels of prophecy. Prophesying for financial gain is a severe temptation that ruins the character of those who prophesy! This will eventually result in a great misuse of the gifting.

Harshness results when an individual steps out of grace into the flesh to prophesy. The result is a harsh spirit coming through the prophetic words given.

A judgmental spirit results when an individual draws from an Old Testament prophet model.

We must desire deeply to avoid these temptations and develop a character that will keep the prophetic flow pure and effective! Let's look at some ways to develop our character in such a way that carries the testimony of Jesus!

- Intimacy with Christ
- Local church accountability
- Ongoing mentoring
- Submitting revelations

- Personal fruit check
- Teachable spirit

Intimacy with Christ is the foundation and most essential part to our character development. Remember the words of Christ,

"I never knew you!" Matthew 7:23

May that not be said of us. Remember, it is His testimony that we are looking to carry in our prophetic gifting!

Local church accountability is imperative. It is important that we all are to be a disciple and under accountability on a local level. This promises the development of true, growing character. I feel so strongly regarding this that I would, in no way, accept the ministry of any prophetic gift that had no accountability.

Ongoing mentoring must continue in the prophetic as this will help form greater character along the journey!

Submitting revelations to constantly check our revelations and words with others brings a safety and character development. Paul even checked his revelation with the apostles in Jerusalem ensuring his doctrine was correct.

Personal Fruit Check: Don't be afraid to personally check the fruit of your character!

A teachable spirit will lead to a great character. In our character development we must ask ourselves, "Do I have a teachable, easily entreated spirit?".

CHAPTER 10
Learning Prophetic Etiquette

As with any walk of life, learning correct etiquette can mean the difference between being received or rejected! The same stands true in the prophetic walk.

> *"And the spirits of the prophets are subject to the prophets."* 1Corinthians 14:32

In other words, God expects us to use correct etiquette in our prophetic ministry. While ministries may differ slightly on their operation of prophetic etiquette, I will discuss some general etiquette on both the personal and public outworking of the prophetic. I never forget as a young man watching my pastor publicly stop someone who tried to jump up and minister while another was talking. He was quick to stop him concerning his lack of etiquette and, actually, plain bad manners. Making no bones that the Holy Spirit was more of a gentleman than he was being given credit for.

Etiquette Regarding Personal Prophecy

You cannot prophesy beyond the will of another person. Each person has the right to receive or reject that which is being prophesied. If an individual is not willing to receive a prophetic word, never force it, just hold your peace! At this point, they are responsible for not receiving the prophetic word!

When prophesying to minors, always have the parents present! This is imperative as parents are responsible for the spiritual welfare of their children. If parents are not available hold the prophecy. Or you may seek the leadership's direction for a ruling in these areas.

If you are prophesying to a lady, always have the husband present. If they are single, always call an elder or trusted leader to witness the word! This is a true safeguard for the giver and the hearer of the prophetic word.

When you are a guest within a house or ministry always gain the permission of the pastor or leader of a house before giving personal prophecy. Seek to be under the covering of leadership within any house or ministry in which you look to prophesy!

If your prophecy has anything of a corrective nature to it always relay these words in private. This is particularly true when the hearer is a leader. Hence, we do not cut across the honor principle and cause carnal people to judge what they have no knowledge of!

On every occasion of personal prophecy make sure there is someone that can hear and judge the word. Again, this is essential for safeguarding the prophetic giver and hearer. If an elder, leader or authority figure is not available use a recording device as a last option!

As you minister to folks try to keep your eyes open. This generally makes people feel far more comfortable when you are ministering to them. Also, you can be aware of their reactions during the ministry.

Never go beyond your gifting or revelation. Do not be tempted to say more than you've been given. Equally, do not try to presume that you have the answers to what you are receiving.

Try to maintain appropriate appearance and hygiene. Many times people are not able to receive due to inappropriate dress or unclean hygiene.

Etiquette Regarding Public Prophecy

1 Corinthians 14 covers the public outworking of prophecy extremely well, but here are a few pointers that will benefit.

Always move with the flow of the Holy Spirit in a particular meeting. In this I mean an individual may receive a legitimate word but the timing to release such a word is of the essence. Never, ever cut across the flow of the Holy Spirit in a meeting.

Look to operate in an orderly fashion. Check the procedure of the particular ministry or church you are in. Always honor the leader of that house or ministry! Many churches have a microphone set up and a designated leader to check words for the prophetic flow.

Be submissive! 1Corinthians 14 makes it so clear that in the prophetic we must always be submissive to one another!

Stay within the measure of your gift! Only give what you have and do not have the need to impress or gain some type of response.

Use your own personality! Avoid the dangerous trap of trying to imitate some other popular prophetic personality! Just simply be yourself.

Again, if possible, always minister with your eyes open. This relays concern for those to whom you're ministering.

CHAPTER 11
Responding to a Word from God

We will only be able to fully realize the power of the prophetic when we learn to correctly respond to a word from God! Let me underscore some incredibly important points regarding words from God!

- We must fully understand the critical need to have God speak His word to us
- Words from God are the basis of our faith
- Words from God must be heard

We must fully understand the critical need to have God speak His word to us!

> *"He humbled you, causing you to hunger and then feeding you with manna, ..., to teach you that man does not live on bread alone but on every word that comes from the mouth of the Lord."*
> Deuteronomy 8:3

Simply, God's word to us is our very life source! This is why the prophetic word of the Lord is so important! Words from God are the basis of our faith!

> *"...faith comes by hearing and hearing by the word of God."* Romans 10:17

The Greek word for *word* in this scripture is *rhema* meaning *an utterance from God.* This is to be differentiated from the Greek word *logos* which has more of a general sense. Faith is simply based on what God says to you!

Words from God must be heard! You cannot respond to what you do not hear. So important is hearing that it warrants a broader discussion. The rest of this chapter is dedicated to the subject. As Jesus would address the church in the book of Revelation he would constantly repeat the phrase, "He that has an ear let him hear what the Spirit is saying to the churches." It is imperative that we have and hone a listening ear to what God is releasing!

Several times in the book of Hebrews this statement is made.

> *"Today if you hear His voice, do not harden your hearts…"* Hebrews 3:7 and Hebrews 4:7

The emphasis of repetition demands investigation. There are several imperative statements!

- Today
- If you hear
- His voice

Today

Let's look closely. *Today* is a present tense word. What is good about it is that as every day passes another *today* appears. It ties in so strongly to the prayer called the Lord's Prayer.

> *"...Give us today our daily bread."* Matthew 6:11

Notice, this is every day! But what is bread?

> *"I am the bread of life."* John 6:48

> *"I am the living bread that came down from heaven. Whoever eats this bread will live forever. This bread is my flesh, which I will give for the life of the world."* John 6:51

If Jesus is the bread of life and the breaking of bread can speak not only of his body but of his word then the impartation of his life and word can come daily. I want what Jesus is breaking and wanting to give me daily! This also speaks to the children of Israel collecting manna daily in Exodus 16!

If You Hear

It becomes your word *if you hear*! Again, the emphasis is on the fact that we must hear! The whole premise of this great statement is that he speaks and does so daily but will we hear it? I believe that we need to do several things in order to hear.

- Set our hearts to listen.
    - *"Give ear and come to me; listen, that you may live."* Isaiah 55:3
- Make it more important than natural things
    - *"Listen, listen to me, and eat what is good, and you will delight in the richest of fare."* Isaiah 55:2
- Read the word of God (*logos*) constantly. It is all his voice and you will develop an ear to hear.
- Listen to the preached word.
- Spend time in prayer. It will release communion with the Holy Spirit.
- Spend time in worship. It is where he sits.
    - *"Yet you are enthroned as the Holy One; you are the one Israel praises."* Psalm 22:3
- Be around the prophetic. What is important about this is that we are, according to Ephesians 4, equipped by the five-fold ministries of Christ. The prophetic trains on hearing and ministering the word of God.

Now look at the response written in the same verse. The response is also the key to the hearing! *"Do not harden your hearts."* If we soften our hearts we will hear and we will respond correctly.

His Voice

Next we look at *His voice*. He speaks constantly and can actually speak to us daily. Whether his voice is released to us once a day or once a week, he has told us,

> *"Man cannot live by bread alone, but by every word that comes from the mouth of God."*
> Deuteronomy 8:3.

The creative word of God! The word of God that sustains! The life-giving word of God! As we have stated, faith comes when we hear the voice of God according to Romans 10:17. We have mentioned the word *rhema*: that particular word to us, that word that we hear. The word that becomes our word!

Sometimes one verse is packed with prophetic explosives. This verse is one such verse. In some ways it sums up so much of the prophetic. He speaks! We listen. We hear and after that we are challenged as to our response!

Let me now give you some very simple but extremely powerful ways to respond to the voice of God through the prophetic!

- Test all things
- Hold on to what you hear
- Follow the word

- Fight for the word
- Mix the word with faith
- Do what we hear

Test all things that come in the realm of prophecy. It is essential that we learn this.

> *"Test everything. Hold on to the good. Avoid every kind of evil."* 1Thessalonians 5:21

> Here are a few methods that will help us *test* prophecy with a right spirit:
> o Use inner witness of the precious Holy Spirit.
> > *"The Spirit himself testifies with our spirit that we are God's children."* Romans 8:16
> o Use the Word of God. Does it line up with the Word?
> o Speak to other prophetic ministries regarding the Word!
> > *"Two or three prophets should speak, and the others should weigh carefully what is said."* 1Corinthians 14:29
> o Do you sense the Spirit of Jesus in it?
> > *"...For it is the Spirit of prophecy who bears testimony to Jesus."* Revelation 19:10

Next learn to hold on to what you know to be God speaking.

> o Hold on to the promise of the Word!

- o Guard the Word you have been given! 1Timothy 1:18
- o Pray the Word you have been given.
- o Confess the Word you have been given.

Next we must learn to follow the Word! We must have this type of following in response to Words from God:

> *"From the days of John the Baptist until now, the kingdom of heaven has been subjected to violence, and violent people take it by force."* Matthew 11:12

We must then fight for the Word from God.

> *"Timothy, my son, I am giving you this command in keeping with the prophecies once made about you, so that by recalling them you may fight the battle well…"* 1 Timothy 1:18

We must mix every Word from God with faith. This is the activating element to the Word we have been given!

> *"For we also have had the good news proclaimed to us, just as they did; but the message they heard was of no value to them, because they did not share the faith of those who obeyed."* Hebrews 4:2

Our final step in responding to a word from God is to do what we hear! God demands a response to the words that He gives us. We cannot simply put it on the shelf and see if it works or comes to pass. Remember,

> *"Today if you hear His voice, harden not your hearts."* Hebrews 3:8

Jesus speaks directly to this issue saying,

> *"Be careful how you hear, with what measure you use, it will be measured to you and even more. Whoever has will be given more; whoever does not have, even what he has will be taken from him."* Mark 4:24, 25

These are very strong words from Jesus. It is so imperative that we respond when God speaks to us!

CHAPTER 12
The Violent Take it by Force

"From the days of John the Baptist until now, the kingdom of heaven suffereth violence, and the violent take it by force." Matthew 11:12 KJV

Although this particular truth is mentioned in the Chapter dealing with how to respond to the prophetic, it also stands alone and needs to be followed. Jesus himself makes special mention of what the prophetic does and how we respond.

Here is what he is actually saying: that when John the Baptist released his prophetic ministry it also released a spirit of forcefulness and aggression to grasp what was said.

Firstly, the prophetic comes as a Kingdom release. What does that mean? Hebrews 12:25-28 gives us an insight that causes us to understand what is happening. Verse 25 declares that when God speaks we shouldn't miss it.

> *"See to it that you do not refuse him who speaks."* Hebrews 12:25

It causes the Kingdom to come knocking at our door. These verses use the Greek word *Paralambano* meaning *something that draws near that should be grasped and received.* When the prophetic comes so does a kingdom opportunity to receive it.

Secondly, it stirs up our spirit to want to enforce what we have heard or been promised. The literal translation of Matthew 11:12 is, "Forceful men lay hold of it and enforce its promise." There is nothing passive about the prophetic! It breaks forth from heaven and then our job is to bring it on home by standing on it and wrestling with it and claiming it and naming it, etc. I have a favorite saying. "Just call me Abraham." What does that mean? Claiming what God says is mine and who he says I am.

There is no putting a prophecy on a shelf to see if it will happen, No! Not at all! Rather, God gives us the privilege of being involved by speaking out his intent and purpose and then we wrestle it into being. One friend of mine told me he takes these promises spoken and goes into the heavenly courts with them, reminding God who spoke to them!!

Also, it is good to note that this is a Kingdom of heaven wrestle and has nothing to do with the enemy as he does not belong to this Kingdom. He might try to dissuade and contest but no, this is to do with us wrestling heavenly promises into being!!

What a privilege to be given the opportunity to be a gainer of Kingdom promises! Let's do it! Let's even go back and dust off old promises and declarations to take hold of them again!

CHAPTER 13
Wrong Reactions to the Prophetic

We are warned throughout scripture regarding the wrong reactions to the prophetic. It would serve us well to take heed to these warnings so as to not miss the best God has for us. Let's look at a few briefly:

- The danger of a hardened heart
- Despising the prophetic
- Shipwrecked faith
- Self-deception
- Entertainment mentality

There is danger in a hardened heart. The word warns us that a hardened heart causes God to be provoked!

> *"Today, if you hear his voice, do not harden your hearts…. That is why I was angry with that generation…"* Hebrews 3:7 and 10

Also, a hardened heart cuts us off from the life of God.

> *"They are darkened in their understanding and separated from the life of God because of the ignorance that is in them due to the hardening of their hearts."* Ephesians 4:18

Hardened hearts refuse to listen for differing reasons. These may include having a spirit of unbelief. Perhaps we don't like the vessel God uses to speak the prophetic word. We might just simply believe the word is from man and not from God. Whatever the reason, we must constantly strive to not allow our hearts to become hard!

Despising the prophetic is another wrong reaction. This type of reaction will put out the Holy Spirit's fire.

> *"Do not quench the Spirit. Do not treat prophecies with contempt but test them all; hold on to what is good, reject every kind of evil."*
> 1 Thessalonians 5:19-22

Again, the reasons may vary why folks despise prophecy, but we must keep our hearts free from this. We do not want to enter the arena of

> *"...having a form of Godliness but denying its power."*
> 2 Timothy 3:5

Shipwrecked faith can cause us to react wrongly to a word from God. Many things can cause a person to have their faith literally wrecked, but the overflow will be rejection of God's word!

> *"Timothy, my son, I am giving you this command in keeping with the prophecies once made about you, so that by recalling them you may fight the battle well, holding on to faith and a good conscience,*

> *which some have rejected and so have suffered shipwreck with regard to the faith."* 1Timothy 1:18-19

Flat out disobedience is one of the most powerful wrong responses to a word from God! God's people could not enter their promise of rest because of their spirit of disobedience! This is a sober warning to us!

> *"Who were they who heard and rebelled?...And to whom did God swear that they would never enter his rest if not to those who disobeyed?"* Hebrews 3:16 and 18

Self-deception is yet another of the worst root causes of responding incorrectly to a word from God. James 1:22-25 warns us that a man who only listens but does nothing with the word is self-deceived and forgets what he has heard and seen. We are also promised that, for the man who obeys, that same word brings freedom and blessing. God takes His word very seriously and so should we!

Also, one vile trait we see in America is the entertainment mentality in response to prophecy. Many times folks love to be entertained by the supernatural rather than changed. This is especially true of the prophetic realm and ministry. Folks will often clap prophecy, particularly if it is in regard to revival or the blessing of God. But! We must ask ourselves if we are doing what we have heard.

CHAPTER 14
The Making of a Prophet

Although there are varying degrees of difference in prophetic realms, the shaping of a prophet is good for all to know no matter the realm you may move in. Jesus' first call to the disciples was,

> *"...follow me and I will make you fishers of men."*
> Matthew 4:19

This same Jesus also released to us the five-fold ministry as we clearly see in Ephesians 4. When Jesus calls, He always makes and shapes!

The Call

Some prophets were called before they were born. This is evidenced in the lives of Jeremiah and even John the Baptist. Others, like the prophet Amos, received their calls later in life. Whatever the timing, there will be a clear call to the prophetic office!

It is important to note that this call may come in differing ways. Some may have a vision, some a dream and others the clear word of God. We must realize the higher the calling, the more significant the call will be! As in words from God, so also with calls of God. We must respond! Consider the principle we find in this statement:

"...whom shall I send, who will go for us? And I said, here I am. Send me." Isaiah 6:8

The Anointing *to* the Call / *in* the Call

Elijah was told to anoint Elisha as a prophet in his place. This anointed Elisha *to* the office in 1 Kings 19. However, it was not until some 10 to 15 years later that Elisha would be anointed *in* the office in 2 Kings 2. The same was true of King David. He would be anointed *to* the kingship in 1 Samuel 16:13, but then *in* the kingship in 2 Samuel 2:5. This is an important principle of God's method in the anointing.

The Training of a Prophet

These are the training grounds of a prophetic ministry:

- Servanthood
- Persecution
- Attack from others
- Loneliness
- The shaping of God
- The training of the Word of the Lord

Servanthood is one of the main training grounds of a prophetic ministry. We see this clearly lived out in the lives of David to Saul, Elisha to Elijah, and Joshua to Moses. Due to the high calling and potential to pride, a prophet must be trained in servanthood.

Persecution will often follow a prophet in his or her call, so they will need to learn to walk this early in their training. Clearly, David and Elisha underwent this type of thing in their ministries.

Attack from others will occur in the prophetic call. Take for instance David being attack viciously by King Saul. Also, note Joseph's betrayal by his brothers as another example.

Loneliness is prevalent in the prophet's life.

The shaping of God many times will involve the issues of obscurity. We are told,

> *"In the hollow of His Hand He hid me; He made me like a polished arrow and concealed me in His quiver."* Isaiah 49:2

Equally, in His polishing we find that God rubs off the rough but He does it with His anointing oil! Then He sharpens you, honing the prophetic gift that He has entrusted to you!

Last and of great value is The Training of the Word of the Lord. We are told that,

> *"…until the word that Joseph spoke came to pass, God used that word to try him."* Psalms 105:19

The Hebrew word here for *try* means *to refine*! The words Joseph spoke had to be refined in him. One rendering of this scripture tells us that the refinement was to put steel in his back. God uses the prophetic on the prophetic so that they will become the very vessels that fulfill their calling!

CHAPTER 15
The Arch Enemy of the Prophetic

The enemy has a particular hatred toward the prophetic and the scripture teaches us that one spirit in particular wars against it viciously! That spirit is known as jezebel! This spirit is cunning and vile and must be stood against. Let's briefly discuss this spirit's schemes and devices.

Jezebel's Desires
At its heart this jezebel spirit looks to rule and control. It will attempt to achieve this by almost any means possible. Its motive is always rule, power and control.

Jezebel's Methods

- It will marry itself to leadership in its attempt to gain control. Jezebel married Ahab in 1 Kings 16:31.

- It will attempt to use intimidation. Jezebel threatens Elijah in 1 Kings 19:2.

- It will always use manipulation to get its own way! Jezebel used this method to gain Naboth's vineyard in 1 Kings 21.

- It will use control to destroy anything in its way. Particularly evil is its attempt to destroy the prophet! 1 Kings 18:4

- It calls itself a prophetess. Revelation 2:20

- It will use adultery to have its own way!

- It will cause others to become idolatrous in its scheming.

Ways to Detect the Jezebel Spirit

- It will always try to find an Ahab to use.

- It will attempt to remove other leaders that stand in its way.

- It will fight the prophets due to their ability to expose its character.

- Always wants a seat next to the leader. Again, looking to gain control or power.

- It likes to gain a teaching place. Revelation 2:20

- It is often engaged in sexual promiscuity. Sometimes this may be spiritual adultery. Revelation 2:20

- It will attempt to produce children after itself. Revelation 2:23

- It will always have an unrepentant heart. Revelation 2:21

- It will always accuse others of being jezebels to stay hidden.

Jezebel's Great Hatred

Jezebel's great hatred is the prophets themselves. This spirit will use any weapon in its arsenal to destroy, defame or sexually entice them. This is its goal: it must remove true prophetic ministry to accomplish its vile purposes.

Jezebel's Defeat

- This spirit is defeated by the word of the Lord. 1Kings 21:23 This is another reason why jezebel looks to remove the prophets. Prophets functioning mean jezebel's ultimate defeat.

- Jezebel's defeat will always come as eunuchs (those given solely to the Lord) throw this spirit down. 2 Kings 9:32,33

It is important to note that although the jezebel spirit has a female gender it can often be a male that is used. I have personally encountered both through the years. Whatever the gender, the signs will always be the same.

CHAPTER 16
Keys to a Prophetic Lifestyle

As previously mentioned at the beginning of this book, the Holy Spirit is the agent of the prophetic: The Revealer himself!

We are told twice in the New Testament that we can have fellowship with the Holy Spirit. Paul tells us that we are all subjects of his fellowship.

> *"May the grace of the Lord Jesus Christ, and the love of God, and the fellowship of the Holy Spirit be with you all."* 2 Corinthians 13:14

In Philippians the statement is made,

> *" If there be…any fellowship of the Spirit."* Philippians 2:1

This statement means fellowship is our privilege but also our option. If we are to walk in the prophetic we must develop a relationship and partnership with the Holy Spirit. The closer we walk, the more we will see and hear! As it is so clearly stated in every one of the letters to the churches in the Book of Revelation, "He that has an ear, let him hear what the Spirit is saying to the churches."

In my own life, some of the greatest encounters from the Lord have been as I cried to know the Holy Spirit. Know him not just for what he does but for who he is. There is no sweeter fellowship than fellowship with him!

It is proved by Elisha in 2 Kings 3, that worship is the key to a spirit in touch with God. "Bring me a minstrel", he said. "I need worship!" Yes, we do. There is nothing like worship to open our hearts to the flow of God, nothing like worship to purify our hearts before God and nothing like worship to keep us close to God! Develop a worship lifestyle.

I used to know a prophet in Little Rock, Arkansas who would pray out loud in tongues before he prophesied. Sometimes he did so in very public places! I know just what he was doing. We are told that he who speaks in an unknown tongue edifies himself.

> *"Anyone who speaks in a tongue edifies themselves..."* 1 Corinthians 14:4

Edify is a great King James word for *builds himself up*! The truer meaning is *builds a house for God to inhabit*! The language of the Spirit indeed. This is a great practice to create a Spirit led life.

Truthfully, the key to the prophetic is an intimate lifestyle with the Lord. It keeps you pure, soft and open. It stops pride and makes a vessel that the Lord can touch and use.

Another great key is found in Proverbs:

> *"As iron sharpens iron, so one person sharpens another."* Proverbs 27:17

Iron sharpens iron means *one should hang around, fellowship and walk with people who operate in the same gifting.* It is amazing how that will enhance the flow in your life. That is why 1 Corinthians 14 speaks of things being revealed to prophets while another one speaks. The prophetic enhances the prophetic!

CHAPTER 17
The Ways of God

In Isaiah 55 (which by the way is a prophet's dream chapter) there is a revelation given by the Lord that all should take note of if they are wanting to understand the prophetic.

> *"'For my thoughts are not your thoughts, neither are your ways my ways,' declares the Lord. 'As the heavens are higher than the earth, so are my ways higher than your ways and my thoughts higher than your thoughts.'"* Isaiah 55:8-9

This statement, coming in a prophetic book and an incredibly prophetic chapter, is worth taking note of but what comes next is the key to understanding much of the prophetic. The Lord links this statement to the prophetic word of the Lord and shows how he does it. He says,

> *"'As the rain and the snow come down from heaven, and do not return to it without watering the earth and making it bud and flourish, so that it yields seed for the sower and bread for the eater, so is my word that comes out of my mouth.'"* Isaiah 55:10-11

He pours it out like rain and snow to water the earth, and also meaning our lives that came from the dust of the earth.

In summary, God from his thoughts and his ways, releases his word from his mouth, to touch and minister to our lives. Like when the Lord renamed Abram to Abraham in Genesis 17 and renamed Jacob to Israel in Genesis 32. He effectively says to them "You call yourself this but I call you this. You see this. But I see this! See what I see and say what I say"!

The intention of the Lord releasing the prophetic is always for change. We saw that Isaiah 55:10 says it causes the earth to bud and flourish and bring forth. So, God releases his word from his ways and thoughts so that the hearer is nurtured and brings forth the fruit they were intended to. Awesome indeed.

Now let's add another dimension from this great chapter! Verse 11 says the word sent from his mouth will not return to him empty but will accomplish what he desires and achieve the purpose for which he sent it.

- He speaks from his ways and thoughts.
- He speaks from his desires for us.
- He releases his words to accomplish what he desires, which means he trusts in the power of his own word to accomplish.
- His purpose is involved for our lives.
- He knows it will work.

Wow, now that gives us added incentive to release and hear the word of God.

He mentioned rain and snow watering the earth which means the life of the Spirit goes with the word and imparts it to touch our lives. The word shows us that when we receive the word of God, it starts working in us.

> *"...when you received the word of God, which you heard from us, you accepted it not as a human word, but as it actually is, the word of God, which is indeed at work in you who believe."* 1 Thessalonians 2:13

I like the King James Version here. "...it effectually worketh". The word here is *energeo* which means *the divine energy of God* is released. If you want to know how powerful this word is, it is the same word mentioned in Ephesians 1:19 when God raised Jesus from the dead. His word received waters our lives by the Spirit and brings all his energy working in us to bring about his intentions and desires!

CONCLUSION

The prophetic is not going away. It is not a phase the church is going through. It was there at the beginning in the book of Genesis and it was there in the early church. It has always been there even when men tried to silence it. But today it is enhancing as God continues to restore his work in the earth. My prayer is that this book might help in the training and sharpening of the prophetic and give us tools to walk in it. Let the genuine be increased and the false revealed. Always we must remember that the prophetic starts with God and finishes with Him. He reveals and he accomplishes as the Book of Isaiah, so clearly says.

> *"Long ago I spoke it and suddenly I act and bring them to pass."* Isaiah 48:3

Our joy is to be part of the process. May we grow together!

Grace to all that read this and are encouraged by it.

TESTIMONIES

"I met Dennis at Peterborough Bible Week many years ago. During the years that I have known Dennis, not only is he a great friend and man of God, but the prophetic apostolic calling on his life is unique. This incisive, accurate, biblical, prophetic gift not only changes people's lives, but brings tremendous biblical guidance to the government of any local church. Both my wife and I highly recommend Dennis' ministry to any emerging apostolic leadership, local church pastors, and to all those that have a heart of the kingdom. He has been invaluable to the life of our church and our people."   -Steve Maile

"This message comes from a very grateful heart ... a couple years ago, my husband Theo and I were attending Oasis and Pastor Dennis prayed for us to have a baby and prophesied that he could see it growing in my womb. I had a struggle with my faith as we had been trying to conceive for several years without success and I was starting to give up hope. But knowing that God isn't a liar, we held fast to that word, and this month we welcomed our little baby girl, Karina Luna. Thank you for praying for us and releasing faith into our lives and serving as a voice for God's promise. God bless you!"   -Kat S.

"Awesome time (Friday Night, Saturday morning) with Dennis Goldsworthy-Davis. Have not experienced manifestations of the Holy Spirit like that before!! Looking forward to more renewal, revival, restoration Hosea 6:1-3. Bring it on!" -Nigel Reid

BIOGRAPHY

Dennis Paul Goldsworthy-Davis has been blessed to travel extensively throughout the world ministering both apostolically and prophetically to the body of Christ. He operates within a strong governmental prophetic office and frequently sees the Presence of God and the Spirit of Revival break out upon the lives of people. Dennis has equally been graced to relate to many spiritual sons throughout the earth, bringing wisdom, guidance and encouragement.

Born in Southern Ireland and raised in England, Dennis was radically saved from a life of drugs and violence in 1973. Soon after his conversion, he began to operate within his local church where he was fathered spiritually by Bennie Finch, a seasoned apostolic minister. After working in youth ministry Dennis pastored in several areas within the U.K. It was during these pastorates that Dennis began to see profound moves of God in these same venues.

In 1986 Dennis experienced a dramatic shift in his life and ministry. He and his family moved to San Antonio, Texas, to join a vibrant, functioning apostolic team. In 1990 Dennis was commissioned to start Great Grace International Christian Center, a local work in San Antonio. Dennis continues to serve as the Senior Minister of GGICC and heads the formation of the apostolic team in the local house. Presently, Dennis relates to several functioning apostolic ministries. He draws wisdom and accountability from Robert Henderson of Global Reformers, Barry Wissler of HarvestNet International and for many years, Alan Vincent. Each of these carry strong, well-seasoned apostolic offices in their own right.

Dennis has been married to his wife, Christine, since 1973 and has two wonderful daughters and four grandchildren.

Printed in Great Britain
by Amazon